One God, One You

Jase Series Book One

Written by Jason Crabb
Illustrated by Anita DuFalla

Printed in the United States of America   ISBN 978-0-9888994-0-7   www.jasoncrabb.com

Through the Fire, Words and Music by Gerald Crabb, Copyright (c) 1999 MPCA Lehsem Songs, Administered by MPCA Music, LLC, International Copyright Secured. All Rights Reserved. *Reprinted by Permission of Hal Leonard Corporation.*

The JASE Series is dedicated to my girls: my beautiful wife, Shellye,
and our precious daughters, Ashleigh and Emma. You mean the world to me.
With love from our family to yours:
Jason, **A**shleigh, **S**hellye, and **E**mma.

Special thanks to Philip and Tina Morris and Donna Scuderi for your creative input and love of the cause.

Number
1

The 1st Commandment

For Crabb Kids

Love God
more than all,
even crabs
great and small.

1. Love God more than all, even crabs great and small.

2. Friend and crab, while you love them, always see God above them.

3. Don't be crabby toward God. Say His name with your love.

4. God's day of rest is for you — and for your crab, too.

5. All children and crabs, respect Mom and Dad.

6. Don't hurt one another, not a crab or your brother.

7. Crab or person alike: love your husband or wife.

8. Never steal from your brother, your crab, or another.

9. Little boys, girls, and crabs, tell the truth and be glad.

10. Be sure to enjoy your stuff and your crab, not wishing for something your neighbor has.

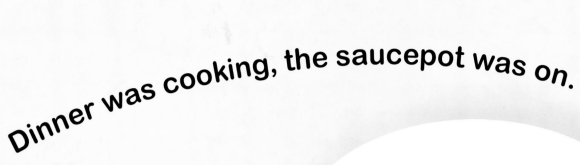

Mom set the table and Ava looked on
while Evan strummed and sang along
with his favorite band and his favorite song.

"Evan … Ava … dinner is ready.
Go wash your hands now, it's time for spaghetti.
And hurry up, we have a surprise.
We'll tell you as soon as your daddy arrives."

"Okay," said Evan, "here we go."
Ava said, "Sketti's my favorite, you know."

Evan scrubbed and wondered, and wondered and scrubbed,
"What in the world will they say when Dad comes?"

"I sure hope it's good, like a toy or a bike

or a day off from school, or a Saturday hike!"

"Yes!" screeched Ava. "A new teddy bear!

I'll have to make room, but I'm not sure where."

When they came to the table, Dad was already there, so they **thanked God in heaven for His loving care.**

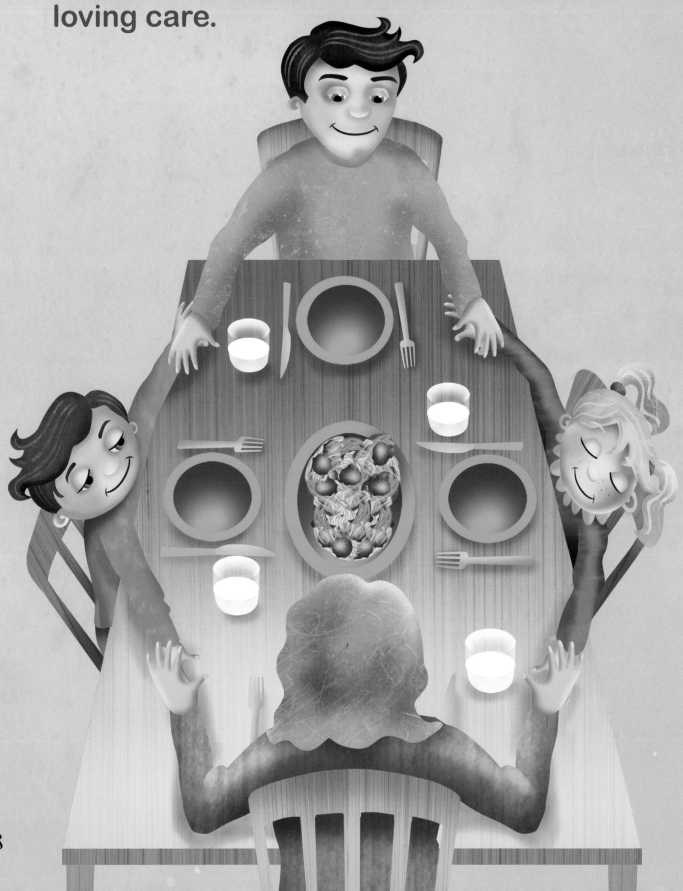

Evan stared at his parents for some little clue
of whatever it was that they already knew.

Then Mom smiled and told him, "I know how you love when a
certain band **worships our God** above."

Evan got still and sucked in his breath, until his mom finally said,
"**Jason Crabb's band** is coming. They're going to play!
They will be here in just a few days."

"For real, Mom? In person?"
"In person," she said.

"Can I bring my **ukulele**?"
Dad nodded his head.

"Thank You, **Jesus**. Thanks Mom and Dad, too! I'm so excited, I'm over the moon!"

The days flew by
and the concert had come.

The whole band played while
Evan strummed.
He sang every note the way they did.

Jason saw him and thought,
"What a talented kid!"

10

He stopped the music and called from the stage, "Buddy, come up here and tell me your name."

Evan could hardly believe it was true. But he ran up the steps, or maybe he flew.

12

"What's your name, little fella?" Jason asked.

"Uhhhh…Evan," he said and almost gasped.

"You have a gift and I have one for you."

"It's *Jase*!" Evan cried, "That is *so* cool! Thank you! Thanks! I can't say it enough," as he smiled really big and gave Jason a hug.

13

The evening's excitement was more than he'd dreamed,
and once in the car Evan dropped off to sleep.
Dad carried him out and up to his bed,
and Mom put Jase right next to his head.

Evan smiled and awakened to hear his dad say,
"Now let's thank God for this wonderful day."

Evan prayed, "Thank, You, God, You are so good.
You blessed us tonight, as You always do.
Thank You for Mom and for Dad and for Jase,
and for Ava, and everything in this whole place.
And thanks for the band being so kind.
May goodness and mercy be all that they find."

15

When the prayer was finished, Evan fell asleep...

… And Jase said, "Hi," in the boy's dream.

When Evan heard him, he was amazed,
and a giant smile splashed across his face.

Excited, he said, "Jase, this is so cool!
I can't wait to tell all my friends back at school."

"If you tell them about me, tell them one special thing —
'Love God more than all, above everything.'"

"That's the first commandment. I know it by heart.
It's not about me. It's all about God."

"That's right!" said Jase. "There is only one God,
and there's only one you who is just as *you* are."

18

Evan wondered, "But God made lots of kids.
He made brothers and sisters
and triplets and twins."

"Yes," Jase explained, "but no two are alike.
For each there's a purpose unique in
God's eyes!"

(Jeremiah 1:5)

"Does that mean, me? Am I unique, too?"

"Yes, and with something special to do.
It's the reason you played and sang with such bliss
while others just *watched* what the band did."

"I see," said Evan, a little bit puzzled …

21

"…Uh-oh," he continued, "Am I in trouble?"

"No, it was awesome!
Would you do it again?
It blesses everyone to no end."

22

"He never promised that the cross would not get heavy,

And the hill would not be hard to climb.
He never offered our victories without fighting,
But he said help would always come in time."

Jase watched Evan, as Jason had done,
and saw the great gift
in this little one.

"Evan, you're gifted and others are too,
who love to worship more than most do.
None has a gift exactly like yours.
Some love arithmetic. Some love to draw.
Some grow up to be chefs or farmers.
Others become mechanics or doctors."

24

"There's so much more,
but I need a snack.
Some cookies and milk
would take care of that."

Evan agreed, "Let's
race to the fridge!"

"No fair!" Jase squealed.
"Your legs are so big!"

Between sloshes of milk and big gooey bites,
Evan slurped and asked, "What happened tonight?
Are you saying my gift is something much more
and God has something special in store?"

"Yes, and it brings blessing to all —
to God and to others because of the call.
Everyone likes music, but not like you do.
It's there for a reason that's special and true."

26

All of a sudden, they both had to laugh
when they saw each other's milky mustache.

With a firm but hilarious, mustachey face
Evan said, "My singing is not all that great.
My ukulele is plastic and the lyrics escape me.
I'm not exactly what I'd call amazing."

With a gentle touch, Jase
said, "That's okay.
Becoming a singer takes
more than a day.
Little by little your voice
gets stronger, and the
songs you remember get
longer and longer.

But always, you'll sing like all singers do,
and **all the rest comes from what God will do:**
A real guitar, and places to sing…
He will help you *with everything*!"

Evan's heart leaped when he heard what Jase said.
And he knew it was right, with his heart, not his head.

"Jase, do you think God would do that for me?
Could I sing on stage like them someday?"

Jase answered and said,
"Not like them, but like you."
Evan looked sad, but Jase
knew what to do.

"Listen," he said, "that's a good thing!
Only *your* voice knows *your* way to sing.
You can learn from others, but you're one of a kind.
Your voice is different from theirs or mine."

"That's awesome, Jase —

one God and one me!

There's no one the same, no one better to be."

"The same thing is true of your mom and your dad, and your sister, Ava —"

"And YOU, Mr. Crabb!"

Jase looked in the mirror and laughed and then twirled.
"There's no other crab like me in this world!"

They laughed so much harder than ever before,
but Evan knew there was still something more.
"Other kids need to know how special they are —
the kids from next door and those from afar!"

"Now you've caught on, you have the gist.
This is the heart of *my* God-given gift.
So, yes, I'll move on, but where I don't know."

"I have an idea. Take my hand and let's go …"

Jase® — A "Crabb" With a Mission

Children are precious — to us and to God! And their growing-up years are so important to the people they become. Through their everyday experiences, children discover their individual identities, their unique destinies, and the reality of their loving Creator.

When faced with challenges and disappointments, children are comforted to learn that other children share many of the same experiences. As they hear other children's stories, they are strengthened in discovering that they are not alone, or "more strange," or "less courageous" than their peers.

The vision for The Jase® Series took root in my heart two decades ago. Now, as a husband and the father of two beautiful girls, I long to reach children and those who love and care for them with the Good News—the gospel of Jesus Christ! I pray that this children's story will sing the melody of God's heart to you, whatever your age.

— Jason Crabb

coming up next in the Jase series

Jesus + You = Two

In a continuing dreamland adventure, Jase® and a new friend, Maya, board Noah's Ark. Jase® teaches Maya that she is never alone … and every storm comes to an end.

Hey kids!

Now that you've read the book, how would you like to:

- Download Jase FUN pages;
- Access the Jase and You Review
- Earn a diploma from Jase University
- And more ...

Go with me to **www.jasecrabb.com** to continue our journey together!!!